TEAM SPIRIT ®

SMART BOOKS FOR YOUNG FANS

THE MIAMI HEAT

BY
MARK STEWART

NORWOODHOUSE PRESS
CHICAGO, ILLINOIS

Norwood House Press
P.O. Box 316598
Chicago, Illinois 60631

For information regarding Norwood House Press, please visit our website at:
www.norwoodhousepress.com or call 866-565-2900.

All photos courtesy of Associated Press except the following:
Topps, Inc. (6, 15, 21, 45), TIME Inc./Sports Illustrated (11), SkyBox International (23),
Author's Collection (29), Miami Heat (33, 34), JBC/NBA Hoops (42 top),
Beckett Publications (42 bottom, 43 top), WinCraft, Inc. (42 right).
Cover Photo: Lynn Sladky/Associated Press

The memorabilia and artifacts pictured in this book are presented for educational and informational purposes,
and come from the collection of the author.

Editor: Mike Kennedy
Designer: Ron Jaffe
Project Management: Black Book Partners, LLC.
Special thanks to Topps, Inc.

Library of Congress Cataloging-in-Publication Data

Stewart, Mark, 1960 July 7-
   The Miami Heat / by Mark Stewart. -- [Revised edition]
       pages cm. -- (Team spirit)
   Includes bibliographical references and index.
   Summary: "A revised Team Spirit Basketball edition featuring the Miami
Heat that chronicles the history and accomplishments of the team. Includes
access to the Team Spirit website which provides additional information and
photos"-- Provided by publisher.
   ISBN 978-1-59953-636-1 (library edition : alk. paper) -- ISBN
978-1-60357-645-1 (ebook)
   1. Miami Heat (Basketball team)--Juvenile literature. I. Title.
   GV885.52.M53S84 2014
   796.323'6409759381--dc23
                                            2014006885

253N—072014
Manufactured in the United States of America in North Mankato, Minnesota.

COVER PHOTO: Team spirit is always on display when the Heat take the court.

Table of Contents

ABOUT OUR GLOSSARY

In this book, there may be several words that you are reading for the first time. Some are sports words, some are new vocabulary words, and some are familiar words that are used in an unusual way. All of these words are defined on page 46. Throughout the book, sports words appear in **bold type**. Regular vocabulary words appear in ***bold italic type***.

Meet the Heat

There are many ways to build a basketball team. The Miami Heat have enjoyed their greatest success when they find two superstars and then surround them with smart, unselfish teammates. Making this *strategy* work isn't as easy as it sounds. It took the Heat almost two *decades* to win their first championship.

For many years, the Heat believed that a little talent and a lot of toughness would lead them to a championship. They came close—and won millions of fans in the process. But in the end, they decided that "star power" was the way to go.

This book tells the story of the Heat. They work hard, play hard, and dream hard. Miami's players and fans are never satisfied. Each season, they are prepared to do whatever it takes to win a championship.

Chris Bosh congratulates LeBron James after a good play. They helped the Heat win back-to-back championships.

Glory Days

Basketball was invented in Massachusetts in the 1890s as a sport that could be played indoors during the winter. A *century* later, the game was being played 365 days a year, inside and outside, all over the United States and all over the world. During the 1980s, the **National Basketball Association (NBA)** announced that it would place a new team in Florida, a state where many people go to escape winter weather. The Miami Heat joined the league for the 1988–89 season.

The Heat struggled, losing their first 17 games in a row. No team in any sport had ever started so poorly. Miami improved as the season went on, but the team finished with just 15 victories. There was one good thing about being so bad. In the NBA, the teams that lose the most get the top picks in the **draft** each spring. Over the next few years, the Heat were able to build a competitive roster. Their young stars included Glen Rice, Steve Smith, Grant Long, Sherman Douglas, and Rony Seikaly.

The final pieces of the puzzle came together during the 1995–96 season. Pat Riley was hired to coach the Heat, and center Alonzo Mourning joined the team and became the leader on the court. Midway through the season, Miami traded for Tim Hardaway, a lightning-quick point guard with a knack for making big shots. The following season, the Heat won 61 games and fell just short of making it to the **NBA Finals**.

Once the Heat found a winning

formula, they began to add players who fit in with their style. They won by playing rugged defense and wearing down their opponents. Their victories were not always "pretty," but Heat fans appreciated their hard-working players. When opponents came to Miami, they knew they would be in for the fight of their lives. Over the next few

LEFT: Rony Seikaly starred for the Heat in their early years.
ABOVE: Alonzo Mourning fit in perfectly with Miami's rugged defensive style.

years, the Heat continued to seek the right mix of players for their first championship.

In 2003, Miami drafted guard Dwyane Wade. He developed into one of the NBA's best all-around players. In 2004, Miami traded for center Shaquille O'Neal, who proved to be a great match for Wade. This pair led Miami to 59 wins in 2004–05. In the **playoffs**, the Heat pushed the Detroit Pistons to Game 7 of the finals of the **Eastern Conference**.

They led the deciding game with three minutes left, but the Pistons came back to win.

A few weeks later, the Heat were part of the biggest trade in league history. Five teams exchanged 13 players. Miami picked up Antoine Walker, James Posey, and Jason Williams. The team also signed **veteran** Gary Payton. Finally, the Heat had the winning combination. Riley returned to the sidelines to coach the team, and Miami went all the way to the NBA Finals. The Heat defeated the

LEFT: Shaquille O'Neal and Dwyane Wade led the Heat to their first championship.   **ABOVE**: Pat Riley's return to the sidelines was another key to Miami's 2006 title.

Dallas Mavericks in six games. Wade was magnificent in the series and was voted **Most Valuable Player (MVP)**.

After their championship season, the Heat continued to tinker with their roster. They traded O'Neal during the 2007–08 season, hoping to energize the team. Soon, Miami realized that Wade needed help carrying the load.

In 2010, the Heat made headlines by signing LeBron James. Many fans considered him to be the best player in the NBA.

James then helped recruit **All-Star** Chris Bosh to Miami. The Heat made another smart move when they drafted point guard Mario Chalmers. Erik Spoelstra was also hired to replace Riley, who continued to lead the team off the court. With the "Big Three" of Wade, James, and Bosh leading the way, Miami returned to the NBA Finals

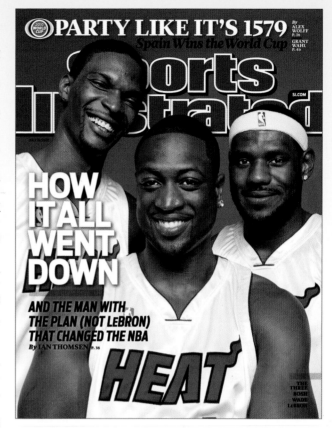

in the spring of 2011 but lost in a rematch with the Mavericks.

Miami continued adding support players, including Mike Miller, Shane Battier, Rashard Lewis, Norris Cole, and Ray Allen. In 2011–12, the Heat were crowned NBA champions. They repeated as champs the following year. At one point during that season, the team won 27 games in a row. With a championship *tradition* and *culture* of success, the Heat should continue to keep Miami fans on the edge of their seats for years to come.

LEFT: LeBron James turned the Heat into a powerhouse. **ABOVE**: The formation of Miami's "Big Three" was front-page news in the sports world.

Home Court

The Heat played their first 10 seasons in the Miami Arena, which was famous for its pink walls. In 2000, the Heat moved three blocks away to a brand new arena. It opened on New Year's Eve with a concert by Gloria Estefan. The Heat played their first game there two days later and beat the Orlando Magic.

Miami's arena is also known as a great place to watch movies, music shows, and plays. Located inside the building is the Waterfront Theater, which can seat nearly 6,000 people. Fans can get to the arena easily by using the Metrorail system.

BY THE NUMBERS

- The Heat's arena has 19,600 seats for basketball.
- The arena cost $213 million to build.
- As of 2013–14, the Heat had retired two jersey numbers: 10 (Tim Hardaway) and 33 (Alonzo Mourning).

The celebration is on in Miami's arena after the team's 2012 championship.

Dressed for Success

The Heat's colors are black, red, and white. They have used them since their first season. At home, the team wears white jerseys and shorts. On the road, they wear black jerseys and shorts. Miami also has red uniforms that are saved for special occasions.

The team's *logo* is easy to recognize. It has always been very "hot." The logo shows a flaming basketball going through a hoop. The flames are done in gold, which is a fourth color that can be found on the Miami uniform. In addition, the *T* in *HEAT* has flames trailing off it. Miami's shorts feature a different version of the logo. They use the letters *MH*, which stand for Miami Heat.

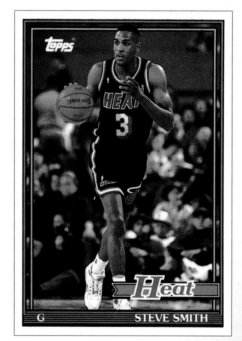

LEFT: Mario Chalmers wears Miami's red uniform during the 2013–14 season. His shorts show an alternate logo.   **ABOVE**: This trading card shows Steve Smith in the team's uniform of the early 1990s.

We Won!

The Heat won their first championship in 2005–06. Shaquille O'Neal and Dwyane Wade were the team's two dynamic leaders. Coach Pat Riley surrounded them with a talented supporting cast that included Jason Williams, James Posey, Gary Payton, Udonis Haslem, and Antoine Walker. Alonzo Mourning backed up O'Neal at center. The Heat survived tense matchups with the Chicago Bulls, New Jersey Nets, and Detroit Pistons to set up a showdown with the Dallas Mavericks in the NBA Finals.

The Mavs swarmed around O'Neal and kept the pressure on Wade, who was limping on a sore knee. Dallas won the first two games at home, and continued to play well in Miami in Game 3. The Mavericks were ahead by 13 points in the fourth quarter, but the Heat came back to win, 98–96. Wade was the hero with 42 points. Miami won Game 4 to even the series, and took Game 5 in **overtime**. Wade starred again with 43 points, including the game-tying shot in the fourth quarter and the deciding free throws in a 101–100 victory.

Dwyane Wade rises for his game-tying basket in Game 5 against the Mavs.

The entire team was ready for Game 6. Wade scored 36 points—including 11 in the fourth quarter—and Mourning blocked five shots in a 95–92 victory. The Heat celebrated the first NBA title in team history. Wade was named MVP of the series.

Miami's next trip to the NBA Finals came at the end of the 2010–11 season. Everyone expected the Heat to win the championship with LeBron James and Chris Bosh in the lineup. However, Miami faced a familiar opponent, the Mavericks. This time, Dallas got revenge, taking the championship in six games.

Miami's "Big Three" of Wade, James, and Bosh vowed they would not let another title slip through their fingers. During the 2011–12 playoffs, the trio was unstoppable. The Heat beat the New York Knicks and Indiana Pacers in the first two rounds of the playoffs. They faced the Boston Celtics in the **Eastern Conference Finals**. Miami fell behind in the series but stormed back to return to the NBA Finals.

Waiting for the Heat were the young and talented Oklahoma City Thunder. Miami's **postseason** experience proved to be the difference. After the Thunder took Game 1, the Heat won the next four games in a row for their second NBA championship.

In Game 4, James was slowed by leg cramps, but Mario Chalmers stepped up with 25 points, including two fourth-quarter baskets that sealed the 104–98 win. In Game 5, Wade got into early foul trouble. Mike Miller provided a spark by hitting seven of eight **3-pointers**. The Heat tied a record with 14 baskets from beyond the arc. James finished with 26 points, 13 **assists**, and 11 rebounds for a **triple-double**, and was named the series MVP.

The Heat repeated as champions in 2012–13. This time they faced the San Antonio Spurs in the NBA Finals. Unlike the Thunder, the Spurs were loaded with veterans, including all-time greats Tim Duncan and Tony Parker. To no one's surprise, the series went the distance.

Game 6 was a classic contest. The Spurs led by 10 points heading into the fourth quarter, but the Heat refused to lose. Miami dug in on defense and cut the deficit to five points with 28 seconds left. Many Miami fans got up from their seats and began leaving the arena. They should have stayed put. After James made the score 95–92, Ray Allen hit a 3-pointer at the buzzer to send the game into overtime. Many experts consider Allen's shot to be one of the best in NBA history. In

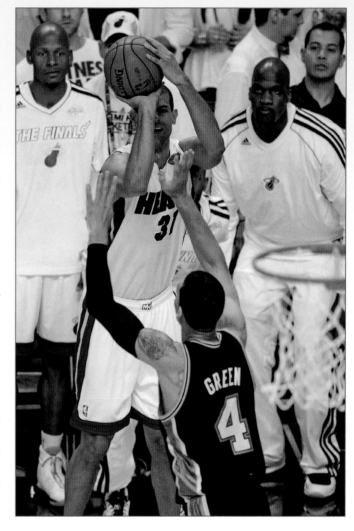

the extra period, Bosh blocked two shots to turn the tide. Miami won to force Game 7.

In the decisive game, the Heat would not be denied. James was magnificent with 37 points. Meanwhile, Battier was on fire from the outside, nailing six 3-pointers. Miami cruised to a 95–88 victory and its third NBA title.

LEFT: LeBron James talks to reporters after Miami's 2012 championship.
ABOVE: Shane Battier lines up a 3-pointer in Game 7 of the 2013 NBA Finals.

Go-To Guys

To be a true star in the NBA, you need more than a great shot. You have to be a "go-to guy"—someone teammates trust to make the winning play when the seconds are ticking away in a big game. Heat fans have had a lot to cheer about over the years, including these great stars …

THE PIONEERS

RONY SEIKALY   6′ 11″ Center

• BORN: 5/10/1965   • PLAYED FOR TEAM: 1988–89 TO 1993–1994

Rony Seikaly was the first player ever taken by the Heat in the NBA draft. He was born in Beirut, Lebanon, and grew up in Greece. He learned to play basketball along the way and became a star for Miami.

GRANT LONG   6′ 9″ Forward

• BORN: 3/12/1966   • PLAYED FOR TEAM: 1988–89 TO 1994–95

For an NBA team to be successful, it needs supporting players who do whatever is asked of them. Grant Long filled that role for the Heat. He scored near the basket, grabbed rebounds against bigger opponents, and played tough defense.

SHERMAN DOUGLAS   6′ 0″ Guard

- BORN: 9/15/1966
- PLAYED FOR TEAM: 1989–90 TO 1991–92

Sherman Douglas was an excellent passer and shooter. But he was at his best leading the fast break. In his second year with the Heat, he led the team in points and assists.

GLEN RICE   6′ 7″ Forward

- BORN: 5/28/1967   • PLAYED FOR TEAM: 1989–90 TO 1994–95

No shot was out of Glen Rice's range, especially beyond the 3-point line. Five times in his six seasons with the Heat, Rice averaged more than 20 points per game. He was named the MVP of the 1997 **All-Star Game**.

ALONZO MOURNING   6′ 10″ Center

- BORN: 2/8/1970
- PLAYED FOR TEAM: 1995–96 TO 2001–02 & 2004–05 TO 2007–08

Alonzo Mourning was a fierce competitor who helped Miami win its first title. He was a great defender and a dangerous scorer. Mourning was named NBA **Defensive Player of the Year** in 1999 and 2000.

TIM HARDAWAY   6′ 0″ Guard

- BORN: 9/1/1966   • PLAYED FOR TEAM: 1995–96 TO 2000–01

Tim Hardaway could change a game with his speed, toughness, and intelligence. When he was hot, he was almost impossible to stop. Hardaway always wanted the ball with the game on the line.

ABOVE: Sherman Douglas

21

DWYANE WADE   6′ 4″ Guard

- BORN: 1/17/1982   • FIRST SEASON WITH TEAM: 2003–04

Dwyane Wade could do it all. He led the NBA with a 30.2 scoring average in 2008–09 and was named the All-Star Game MVP in 2010. Wade was at his best in the playoffs when the Heat needed him the most.

UDONIS HASLEM   6′ 8″ Forward

- BORN: 6/9/1980

- FIRST SEASON WITH TEAM: 2003–04

Udonis Haslem showed just how important a role player is to a championship team. He was a tough rebounder and defender who always focused on winning. Haslem was a key contributor to Miami's three NBA titles.

SHAQUILLE O'NEAL   7′ 1″ Center

- BORN: 3/6/1972

- PLAYED FOR TEAM: 2004–05 TO 2006–07

When the Heat traded for Shaquille O'Neal, they hoped his leadership and experience would rub off on his teammates. O'Neal was an All-Star in all three of his seasons in Miami. He helped the team win its first championship in 2006.

MARIO CHALMERS   6′ 2″ Guard

- BORN: 5/18/1986
- FIRST SEASON WITH TEAM: 2008–09

The Heat drafted Mario Chalmers after he led his college team to a national championship. He became Miami's starting point guard as a **rookie** and gave the team a big boost. In 2012–13, he tied Brian Shaw's team record with 10 3-pointers in a game.

CHRIS BOSH   6′ 11″ Forward/Center

- BORN: 3/24/1984   • FIRST SEASON WITH TEAM: 2010–11

Chris Bosh joined the Heat after setting the all-time scoring and rebounding records for the Toronto Raptors. With Miami, Bosh took on more of a defensive role, but he loved taking big shots in tight games. He helped the Heat reach the NBA Finals in each of his first three seasons.

LeBRON JAMES   6′ 8″ Forward

- BORN: 12/30/1984   • FIRST SEASON WITH TEAM: 2010–11

Few players could match the skill and power of LeBron James. He earned two titles in his first three seasons with Miami. He was voted MVP of the NBA Finals both times.

LEFT: Udonis Haslem   **ABOVE**: Mario Chalmers

Calling the Shots

Over the years, South Florida's pleasant climate has attracted some of basketball's best players to the Heat. Not surprisingly, the weather makes Miami an appealing place for coaches, too. Indeed, the Heat have had some of the best in the business. When Billy Cunningham came to Miami, he already had a championship under his belt as a coach. He showed the Heat what it took to be a winning team. Kevin Loughery did the same. He worked for the Heat as a scout before becoming the head coach.

In 1995–96, Pat Riley took over the Heat. Riley had coached the Los Angeles Lakers to four NBA titles in the 1980s, so he knew all about winning championships. He had also been the coach of the New York Knicks, one of Miami's biggest *rivals*. Riley asked his players to share the ball on offense and work together on defense. The Heat won their **division** four years in a row under Riley. In 1996–97, he guided them to their first 60-win season.

Riley retired from coaching for health reasons, but he continued to help run the team. His replacement, Stan Van Gundy, coached

Ray Allen and Erik Spoelstra talk strategy during a timeout.

the Heat to within a single win of the NBA Finals in 2005. When Riley returned to health, he agreed to come back as Miami's coach for the 2005–06 season. That year, he led the Heat to their first championship.

In 2008–09, Riley stepped down again, and Erik Spoelstra took over as coach. Spoelstra was young and energetic. He used technology to his advantage. The Heat improved by 28 wins in his first season! Spoelstra led Miami to the NBA Finals three years in a row. When the Heat won the championship in 2011–12, Spoelstra— who is half-Filipino on his mother's side—became the first Asian American to coach an NBA team to the title.

One Great Day

The mark of a great player is his ability to seize control of important games in the deciding minutes. In Game 7 of the 2013 NBA Finals, LeBron James did just that. Two days earlier, with their backs against the wall, the Heat survived a wild overtime battle with the San Antonio Spurs. Could Miami finish its comeback and win a second NBA title in a row?

Miami held a slim lead when the fourth quarter began. Every time the Heat tried to pull away, the Spurs made a great shot or defensive play. With less than six minutes left and the Heat up by four points, James nailed a jump shot. The Spurs called timeout to talk over strategy. They had to stop James.

That was easier said than done. Over the next five minutes, James connected on two long shots, set up Shane Battier for an open 3-pointer, ripped down three rebounds, made a key steal, and hit a pair of pressure-packed free throws. In all, he scored 37 points and pulled down 12 rebounds. Miami won by seven points.

LeBron James powers to the hoop for an easy basket in Game 7 against the Spurs.

His performance came as no surprise to Miami coach Erik Spoelstra. "He always rises to the occasion when it matters the most, when the competition is fiercest," Spoelstra said.

No one was surprised, either, when James was named the series MVP. He joined all-time greats Larry Bird and Michael Jordan as the only players to win the MVP award for the regular season and for the NBA Finals twice in their careers.

Legend Has It

Did the Heat have the best finish in NBA history?

LEGEND HAS IT that they did. In 2003–04, the team started the season by losing seven games in a row. When the month of March began, they had 11 more losses than wins. Many fans gave up on the season. But the Heat did not. Led by rookie Dwyane Wade and veteran Eddie Jones, the Heat got red-hot and won 17 of their last 21 games. They ended up at 42–40. No team had ever come so far—so fast—to finish with a winning record.

ABOVE: Eddie Jones was one of the keys to Miami's incredible turnaround during the 2003–04 season.
RIGHT: This sheet of postage stamps features Dwyane Wade.

Was Chris Bosh the Heat's top half-court shooter?

LEGEND HAS IT that he was. Normally, a shot of this distance is only tried in desperation, with no time left on the clock. But Bosh put on an amazing display during the 2014 All-Star weekend, when he led a three-person team to victory in the Shooting Stars Competition. During warm-ups he could barely hit the rim. But Bosh took two shots from 47 feet away and made them both.

Which Miami player was featured on a postage stamp?

LEGEND HAS IT that Dwyane Wade was. In 2008, the island nation of Grenada issued a 75-cent stamp that featured the Miami star. Grenada is located in the southeastern Caribbean, near the coast of Venezuela.

It Really Happened

Players in the NBA are trained to overcome any obstacle they face on the court. But what happens when they must fight against a life-threatening illness? In the fall of 2000, Alonzo Mourning found himself in a struggle with kidney disease. The kidneys clean the blood and help the body to work properly. Mourning's kidneys were not working correctly.

No one could believe Mourning was ill. He looked great, and seemed as strong as ever. He had just been named NBA Defensive Player of the Year. Mourning also helped Team USA win a gold medal in men's basketball at the 2000 *Summer Olympics*. Even so, he was a very sick man.

Mourning's doctors tried to treat his disease with medicine. He sat out most of the 2000–01 season, and then tried to play the following year. Mourning's kidneys continued to get worse. He sat out the 2002–03 season, but the rest did not help. He was told that he would die if he did not receive a kidney transplant.

Alonzo Mourning's positive attitude helped him overcome kidney disease—and return to the court for the Heat.

Mourning's teammates knew he was a fighter. They believed that he would win this life-and-death battle. None of them, however, thought he would ever play basketball again. Imagine their surprise when Mourning announced that he was ready to suit up in 2003–04.

Three years after he was diagnosed with kidney disease, Mourning was back on the court as a member of the New Jersey Nets. The following season, when the Heat needed an experienced back-up for Shaquille O'Neal, they made a trade with the Nets. Mourning returned to Miami and helped the Heat win more games than any team in the Eastern Conference.

Team Spirit

The Heat have some of the most loyal and passionate fans in the country. They understand what it takes to win in the NBA, and they let the Heat players know that they appreciate a job well done. Many of Miami's fans are celebrities. Their star power is a great source of pride for the team.

Miami is a *diverse* city. The crowd at a Heat game is a reflection of the people who live in the area. As fans take their seats, you see people who work nine-to-five jobs sitting next to artists, writers, and musicians. You see retired couples chatting with young celebrities. You see sport-fishing captains trading stories with clothing designers. And when the Heat score or make a great defensive play, you see everyone rise to their feet as one.

LEFT: Heat fans cheer LeBron James as he jogs out to the court.
ABOVE: The Heat made this schedule available to their fans for the team's first season.

33

Timeline

The basketball season is played from October through June. That means each season takes place at the end of one year and the beginning of the next. In this timeline, the accomplishments of the Heat are shown by season.

1991–92
The Heat make the playoffs for the first time.

1996–97
The Heat reach the Eastern Conference Finals.

1988–89
The Heat play their first NBA season.

1995–96
Pat Riley becomes Miami's coach.

1998–99
Alonzo Mourning is named Defensive Player of the Year.

Fans bought this souvenir pennant during the Heat's first season.

Dwyane Wade accepts the All-Star MVP trophy from NBA commissioner David Stern.

2003–04
Dwyane Wade makes the **All-Rookie Team**.

2009–10
Dwyane Wade is named MVP of the All-Star Game.

2011–12
The Heat win their second NBA championship

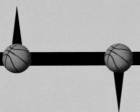

2005–06
The Heat win their first NBA championship.

2012–13
Miami wins its second championship in a row.

James Posey and Antoine Walker celebrate Miami's 2006 championship.

Fun Facts

CRUISE CONTROL

Ted Arison helped bring the Heat to Miami in the 1980s. His son, Mickey, later became the team owner. Their family made their fortune from the Carnival cruise ship business.

FOOTLOOSE

In Game 6 of the 2013 NBA Finals, Mike Miller hit a key 3-pointer in Miami's dramatic fourth-quarter comeback. Moments earlier, Miller had lost his shoe. He made his shot wearing just one shoe.

WHAT A STEAL!

In 2008, the Heat picked Mario Chalmers in the second round of the draft. He won a starting job and led all NBA rookies with 1.95 steals per game. In his fourth game, Chalmers smashed Miami's team record with nine steals against the Philadelphia 76ers.

TRIPLE TROUBLE

The first player in team history to record a triple-double was Steve Smith. He scored 21 points with 12 assists and 10 rebounds in a game during the 1992–93 season.

UNWANTED

In 2003, the Heat signed Udonis Haslem after no other NBA team drafted him. Ten years later, he passed Alonzo Mourning as Miami's all-time leader in rebounds. No undrafted player in history had ever led his team in this category.

OH, WHAT A NIGHT!

In a game in April of 1993 against the Milwaukee Bucks, Brian Shaw hit 10 3-point shots. At the time, it was a league record.

ABOVE: Steve Smith

Talking Basketball

"It's not about the money. It's not about anything else except for winning."
▶ **Chris Bosh,** *on putting team goals before personal goals*

"It took maybe about a year for me, 'Bron, and CB just because they were new players and we all had to get accustomed to each other."
▶ **Mario Chalmers,** *on getting used to working with LeBron James and Chris Bosh*

"Don't point fingers or do the blame game. A team is a family, and we're in this together."
▶ **Erik Spoelstra,** *on the importance of supporting your teammates*

ABOVE: Chris Bosh autographed this photo right after he joined the Heat.
RIGHT: Alonzo Mourning knows all about tough times.

"Tough times don't last, but tough people do."

▶ **Alonzo Mourning,** *on overcoming his battle with kidney disease*

"He's got ice water in his veins. That's just the confidence he has in himself."

▶ **LeBron James,** *on Ray Allen's ability to shoot under pressure*

"LeBron brings out the best in me, and I bring out the best in him."

▶ **Dwyane Wade,** *on LeBron James*

"When I have open looks, I expect to make them. And I did."

▶ **Shane Battier,** *on his six 3-pointers in Game 7 of the 2013 NBA Finals*

Great Debates

People who root for the Heat love to compare their favorite moments, teams, and players. Some debates have been going on for years! How would you settle these classic basketball arguments?

Shaquille O'Neal was Miami's best "post-up" player . . .

... because when he played with his back to the basket, no one could stop him. Shaq (LEFT) used his size and quickness to create havoc on the court. When he got a pass near the hoop, it forced the defense to double-team him. The result was a basket, a foul, or a pass to a wide-open teammate.

LeBron James was even better posting up his man . . .

... because he had a wide assortment of moves. Playing one-on-one close to the basket used to be the weakest part of James's game. After joining the Heat, he began working on this weakness and turned it into a strength. By 2013, James was as dangerous in the post as he was facing the basket. In fact, Miami often ran plays specifically for him near the hoop.

Glen Rice was the Heat's greatest long-distance shooter ...

... because when he got hot, no one was better. In six years with the Heat, Rice (RIGHT) led the team in 3-pointers five times and was second once. In some years, he had more 3-pointers than his next two teammates combined. At the 1995 All-Star Game, Rice out-shot Reggie Miller to win the 3-Point Shootout. Two months later, he scored 56 points in a game.

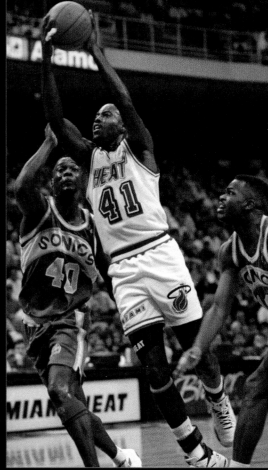

Come on! No one tops Ray Allen ...

... because he hit the most famous 3-pointer in team history. In Game 6 of the 2013 NBA Finals, he nailed a fall-away 3-pointer from the corner to tie the game at the buzzer. His shot forced Game 7, which the Heat won for their third championship. In Allen's first year with Miami, he had the most 3-pointers on a team with four other great long-distance shooters—LeBron James, Mike Miller, Mario Chalmers, and Shane Battier.

For the Record

The great Heat teams and players have left their marks on the record books. These are the "best of the best" …

Rony Seikaly

Harold Miner

HEAT AWARD WINNERS

MOST IMPROVED PLAYER	
Rony Seikaly	1989–90
Isaac Austin	1996–97

SLAM DUNK CHAMPION	
Harold Miner	1992–93
Harold Miner	1994–95

3-POINT SHOOTOUT WINNER	
Glen Rice	1994–95
Daequan Cook	2008–09
James Jones	2010–11

NBA MVP	
LeBron James	2011–12
LeBron James	2012–13

NBA FINALS MVP	
Dwyane Wade	2005–06
LeBron James	2011–12
LeBron James	2012–13

DEFENSIVE PLAYER OF THE YEAR	
Alonzo Mourning	1998–99
Alonzo Mourning	1999–00

ALL-STAR GAME MVP	
Dwyane Wade	2009–10

COACH OF THE YEAR	
Pat Riley	1996–97

Fans celebrated the Heat's 2006 championship with this pennant.

HEAT ACCOMPLISHMENTS

ACHIEVEMENT	SEASON
Atlantic Division Champions	1996–97
Atlantic Division Champions	1997–98
Atlantic Division Champions	1998–99
Atlantic Division Champions	1999–00
Southeast Division Champions	2004–05
Southeast Division Champions	2005–06
Eastern Conference Champions	2005–06
NBA Champions	2005–06
Southeast Division Champions	2006–07
Southeast Division Champions	2010–11
Eastern Conference Champions	2010–11
Southeast Division Champions	2011–12
Eastern Conference Champions	2011–12
NBA Champions	2011–12
Southeast Division Champions	2012–13
Eastern Conference Champions	2012–13
NBA Champions	2012–13
Southeast Division Champions	2013–14

Tim Hardaway averaged more than 17 points a game during his career in Miami. He helped the Heat win their division four years in a row.

Alonzo Mourning was named Defensive Player of the Year twice with the Heat. In this picture, NBA great Bill Russell presents him with one of his trophies.

Pinpoints

The history of a basketball team is made up of many smaller stories. These stories take place all over the map—not just in the city a team calls "home." Match the pushpins on these maps to the **TEAM FACTS**, and you will begin to see the story of the Heat unfold!

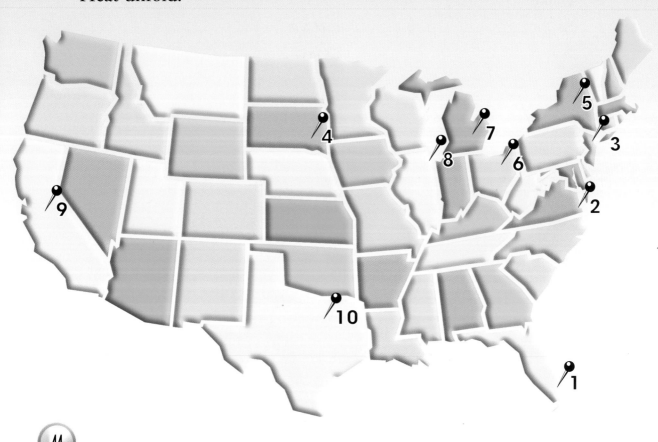

TEAM FACTS

1   Miami, Florida—*The Heat have played here since 1988–89.*

2   Chesapeake, Virginia—*Alonzo Mourning was born here.*

3   Newark, New Jersey—*Shaquille O'Neal was born here.*

4   Mitchell, South Dakota—*Mike Miller was born here.*

5   Rome, New York—*Pat Riley was born here.*

6   Akron, Ohio—*LeBron James was born here.*

7   Flint, Michigan—*Glen Rice was born here.*

8   Chicago, Illinois—*Dwyane Wade was born here.*

9   Merced, California—*Ray Allen was born here.*

10   Dallas, Texas—*Chris Bosh was born here.*

11   Anchorage, Alaska—*Mario Chalmers was born here.*

12   Beirut, Lebanon—*Rony Seikaly was born here.*

Glen Rice

Glossary

3-POINTERS—Shots taken from behind the 3-point line.

ALL-ROOKIE TEAM—The annual honor given to the NBA's best first-year players at each position.

ALL-STAR—A player selected to play in the annual All-Star Game.

ALL-STAR GAME—The annual game in which the best players from the East and the West play against each other.

ASSISTS—Passes that lead to baskets.

CENTURY—A period of 100 years.

CULTURE—A way of thinking and behaving that exists in a place or organization.

DECADES—Periods of 10 years; also specific periods, such as the 1950s.

DEFENSIVE PLAYER OF THE YEAR—The annual award given to the league's best defensive player.

DIVERSE—Representing many cultures.

DIVISION—A group of teams within a league that play in the same part of the country.

DRAFT—The annual meeting during which NBA teams choose from a group of the best college and foreign players.

EASTERN CONFERENCE—A group of teams that play in the East. The winner of the Eastern Conference meets the winner of the Western Conference in the league finals.

EASTERN CONFERENCE FINALS—The playoff series that determines which team from the East will play the best team from the West for the NBA championship.

FORMULA—A set way of doing something.

LOGO—A symbol or design that represents a company or team.

MOST VALUABLE PLAYER (MVP)—The annual award given to the league's best player; also given to the best player in the league finals and All-Star Game.

NATIONAL BASKETBALL ASSOCIATION (NBA)—The professional league that has been operating since 1946–47.

NBA FINALS—The playoff series that decides the champion of the league.

OVERTIME—An extra period played when a game is tied after 48 minutes.

PLAYOFFS—The games played after the season to determine the league champion.

POSTSEASON—Another term for playoffs.

RIVALS—Extremely emotional competitors.

ROOKIE—A player in his first season.

STRATEGY—A plan or method for succeeding.

SUMMER OLYMPICS—An international sports competition held every four years.

TRADITION—A belief or custom that is handed down from generation to generation.

TRIPLE-DOUBLE—A game in which a player records double-figures in three different statistical categories.

VETERAN—A player with great experience.

FAST BREAK

TEAM SPIRIT introduces a great way to stay up to date with your team! Visit our **FAST BREAK** link and get connected to the latest and greatest updates. **FAST BREAK** serves as a young reader's ticket to an exclusive web page—with more stories, fun facts, team records, and photos of the Heat. Content is updated during and after each season. The **FAST BREAK** feature also enables readers to send comments and letters to the author! Log onto:

www.norwoodhousepress.com/library.aspx

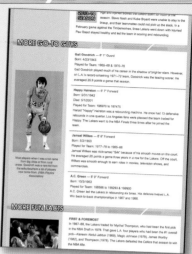

and click on the tab: **TEAM SPIRIT** to access **FAST BREAK**.

Read all the books in the series to learn more about professional sports. For a complete listing of the baseball, basketball, football, and hockey teams in the **TEAM SPIRIT** series, visit our website at:

www.norwoodhousepress.com/library.aspx

On the Road

MIAMI HEAT
601 Biscayne Boulevard
Miami, Florida   33132
(786) 777-1000
www.Heat.com

NAISMITH MEMORIAL BASKETBALL HALL OF FAME
1000 West Columbus Avenue
Springfield, Massachusetts 01105
(877) 4HOOPLA
www.hoophall.com

On the Bookshelf

To learn more about the sport of basketball, look for these books at your library or bookstore:

- Doeden, Matt. *Basketball Legends In the Making*. North Mankato, Minnesota: Capstone Press, 2014.

- Rappaport, Ken. *Basketball's Top 10 Slam Dunkers*. Berkeley Heights, New Jersey: Enslow Publishers, 2013.

- Silverman, Drew. *The NBA Finals*. Minneapolis, Minnesota: ABDO Group, 2013.

Index

THE TEAM

MARK STEWART has written more than 40 books on basketball, and over 150 sports books for kids. He grew up in New York City during the 1960s rooting for the Knicks and Nets, and was lucky enough to meet many of the stars of those teams. Mark comes from a family of writers. His grandfather was Sunday Editor of *The New York Times* and his mother was Articles Editor of *The Ladies' Home Journal* and *McCall's*. Mark has profiled hundreds of athletes over the last 20 years. He has also written several books about his native New York, and New Jersey, his home today. Mark is a graduate of Duke University, with a degree in History. He lives with his daughters and wife Sarah overlooking Sandy Hook, New Jersey.